Krav Maga

Disrupt, Damage, Destroy, Disengage: Practical Solutions to Real World Challenges

Adam Fisher

The following book is reproduced below with the goal of providing information that is as accurate and as reliable as possible. Regardless, purcha-sing this book can be seen as consent to the fact that both the publisher and the author of this book are in no way experts on the topics discussed within, and that any recommendations or suggestions made herein are for entertainment purposes only. Professionals should be consulted as needed before undertaking any of the action endorsed herein.

This declaration is deemed fair and valid by both the American Bar Association and the Committee of Publishers Association and is legally binding throughout the United States.

Furthermore, the transmission, duplication or reproduction of any of the following work, including precise information, will be considered an illegal act, irrespective whether it is done electronically or in print. The legality extends to creating a secondary or tertiary copy of the work or a recorded copy and is only allowed with express written consent of the Publisher. All additional rights are reserved.

The information in the following pages is broadly considered to be a truthful and accurate account of facts, and as such any inattention, use or misuse of the information in question by the reader will render any resulting actions solely under their purview. There are no scenarios in which the publisher or the original author of this work can be in any fashion deemed liable for any hardship or damages that may befall them after undertaking information described herein.

Additionally, the information found on the following pages is intended for informational purposes only and should thus be considered, universal. As befitting its nature, the information presented is without assurance regarding its continued validity or interim quality. Trademarks that are mentioned are done without written consent and can in no way be considered an endorsement from the trademark holder.

Table of Contents

Introduction

Congratulations on downloading your personal copy of *Krav Maga*. Thank you for doing so.

The following chapters will discuss some of the many effective Krav Maga techniques that can help you if you were ever faced with a fight.

You will discover how important your mind is when it comes to confronting and de-escalating a fight. Your mind is the most powerful tool you own. You don't need fancy weapons to win in a fight; you just need smarts and your own body.

The final chapter will provide you with ways to defend yourself in the event of an unarmed attack. It also gives women some tips to defend themselves against an attacker.

There are plenty of books on this subject on the market, thanks again for choosing this one! Every effort was made to ensure it is full of as much useful information as possible. Please enjoy!

Congratulations on downloading your personal copy of *Krav Maga*. Thank you for doing so.

Krav Maga Introduction

Krav Maga is a self-defense technique that was developed by the military of the Israeli security forces of Mossad and Shin Bet and the Israel Defense Forces that combines the techniques of judo, realistic fight training, aikido, wrestling, and boxing. It is known for the way it focuses on real world situations, its brutal counterattacks, and extreme efficiency. It was created by Imre Lichtenfeld. He took his street-fighting experiences from the Hungarian-Israeli martial arts. He used his training as a wrestler and boxer as a way to defend the Jewish quarter in the mid to late 1930s in Bratislava, Czechoslovakia from the fascist groups after he migrated to Israel. He gave lessons in combat training to what became the Israel Defense Forces.

Imre Lichtenfeld also called Imi Sde-Or was born in Budapest, Hungary in 1910 and was raised in Bratislava. He was active in many sports like boxing, wrestling, and gymnastics. He won the Slovak Youth Wrestling Championship in 1928. He won the adult middle and lightweight divisions championship in 1929. He won an international gymnastics and a national boxing championship in the same year. During the same decade, his activities focused on wrestling as a trainer and contestant.

Anti-Semitic riots started threatening the Jews in Bratislava, Czechoslovakia in the middle 1930s. He led a group of Jewish wrestlers and boxers that hit the streets to defend their Jewish neighborhoods against the increasing numbers of the anti-Semitic thugs and the national socialist party. He quickly figured out that street fighting was totally different than competition fighting. Wrestling and boxing were good sports, but they weren't practical for the brutal and aggressive nature of fighting in the streets. He then began to rethink his ideas on fighting and developed the techniques and skills that became Krav Maga. He was a thorn in the side of the anti-Semitic local authorities. He left home, with friends and family on one of the last ships to escape Europe in 1940.

He made his way to Israel and joined Israel's paramilitary to protect the Jewish refugees from the Arabs. He started training fighters in 1944 in his areas of expertise like defense against knife attacks, using a knife, wrestling, swimming, and physical fitness. He also trained many elite units of the Haganah that included the Pal-Yam, police officers, and the Palmach.

Once the State of Israel and the Israeli Defense Forces were formed, he became the Chief Instructor for Krav Maga and Physical Fitness in the Israeli Defense Forces School of Combat Fitness. He served for 20 years. He refined his methods for hand to hand combat and self-defense during this time. Since all martial arts developed some kind of defensive techniques to be the best in dominating the sport, self-defense wasn't new. It was based on the dynamic principle of the human body. Judo training was added as a new Krav Maga technique in 1965. There were not any grades in Krav Maga until 1968. The grades are determined by a trainee's knowledge of judo.

Imi's best student and the very first black belt, Eli Avikzar, started learning Aikido in 1968. He went to France and received a brown belt in Aikido. When he returned, he worked as an instructor beside Imi, and they improved Krav Maga by incorporating counter defenses and Aikido into Krav Maga. Imi retired and turned the Krav Maga training center over to Eli. He soon joined the Israeli Defense Forces as the head of the Krav Maga sector. The use of Krav Maga advanced after Eli took over. The soldiers were given courses, and each Physical Education instructor had to learn Krav Maga. He developed Krav Maga constantly until he retired in 1987. Upon his retirement, he had trained 12,000 female and 80,000 male soldiers.

Eli further pursued his excellence in martial arts by going to Germany and earned a black belt in Aikido in 1977. The Krav Maga association was founded in 1978. Eli helped establish the professional ranks by establishing the Israeli Krav Maga Association in 1989. He retired in 1987 as Chief Krav Maga instructor. Boaz Aviram became the last head instructor that studied with both Avikzar and Lichtenfeld.

The Israeli Defense Forces Krav Maga instructor course takes five weeks to complete.

They hold an annual competition that began in May 2013. Some Krav Maga organizations don't support competitions. They don't look at Krav Maga as a sport. These sports usually operate under safe techniques that do minimal harm. They just wear down their opponents by using tactics that support the rules of safe competition. Krav Maga operates under a set of rules where techniques might cause a lot of damage and conflicts are ended quickly if a conflict can't be avoided within the role of a hand to hand combat and self-defense system. The organizations that include competitions are founded specifically to focus on using Krav Maga specifically for sport.

When Lichtenfeld retired, he opened a school and taught Krav Maga to civilians. In 1971, his first course was at the Wingate Institute in Netanya, Israel. The first people to receive black belts from Lichtenfeld's civilian Krav Maga class were: Miki Assulin, Avner Hazan, Yaron Lichtenstein, Vicktor Bracha, Shlomo Avisira, Haim Hakani, Shmuel Kurzweil, Haim Zut, Meni Ganis, Raphy Elgrissy, Richard Douieb, Eyal Yanilov, Ani Niv Krav Maga Aiki, Eli Avikzar, James Rubenis, and Haim Gidon.

Lichtenfeld created a non-profit Israeli Krav Maga Association with many senior instructors. When he retired, he placed Haim Gidon to be the president and Grand Master of the IKMA. In Netanya, Israel in January 1998, Lichtenfeld died.

Once Krav Maga began to go beyond the borders of Israel, there was a need to establish an international organization. Some of Lichtenfeld's students Dan Levy, Asaf Halevi, and Arviat Zagal formed a new international Krav Maga Federation.

Some of the organizations in Israel like Krav Maga Worldwide, by Darren Levine, Ultimate Survivor Krav Maga International USKMI and international KMW, Alpha Krav Maga, but Sam Sade, Traditional Krav

Maga by Erez Sharabi, Israeli Krav Magen Association by Eli Avikzar Krav Maga Federation by Haim Zut, Bukan by Yaron Lichtenstein, Israeli Krav Maga Association by Haim Gidon, and the Krav Maga Aiki Ami Niv Federation use the original belt grading system that is based on the Judo ranking system. It begins with a white belt. Then a student will earn the yellow. Then they earn the orange. After that comes green, then blue, and the last two are brown and black. Students who receive a black belt can move from first to ninth Dan. The time that is required to be able to advance is different in each organization.

The different organizations that teach Krav Maga in and out of Israel such as International Krav Maga, Krav Maga Global, International Krav Maga Federation, and Krav Maga Aiki Ami Niv Federation all use the grading system of awarding patches. This patch system was created after the belt system of Lichtenfeld's at the end of the 1980s. These are divided into three different categories: Practitioner, Graduate and then Expert. Each has five different ranks. The student levels from P1 to P5 are the majority within the Krav Maga community. The next ranks are G1 to G5. To be able to get to the Graduate levels the student must demonstrate proficiency in every P level technique. Most instructors will hold a G grade and instruct civilians. They have to pass a training course and holding a G rank will not make them an instructor. The Expert grades get into advanced military and protection techniques including advanced fighting and sparring skills. Instructors who hold these tanks usually teach in sectors like law enforcement and military. To get to the expert levels, they have to have proficiency in all the Practitioner and Graduate levels as well as excellent fighting skills. Past the rank of Expert 5 is Master. This is only held by a small number of people and is reserved for those who have dedicated their lives to Krav Maga and have made great contributions to promoting and teaching this style.

Krav Maga organizations in Europe, South America, and the United States like Krav Maga Academy Slovenia, Hagana System, European Federation of Krav Maga, South American Federation of Krav Maga, Krav Maga Street Defense, United States Krav Maga Association, Apolaki Krav Maga, National Krav Maga Association, Fit to Fight, Krav Maga Alliance, and Krav Maga Worldwide use the belt ranking system like Bukan, KMF, and IKMA. Though, there are some differences in each organization they all teach the same principles and techniques. Organizations like Urban Krav Maga and Pure Krav Maga that was founded by Boaz Aviram have grading ranks without patches or belts. They do have levels in which students are able to monitor their progress.

In the organization Krav Maga Global, sparring is light and slow until they reach the level of G2. This will take anywhere from four to six years. Rising just one level in the Practitioner and Graduate levels will take a minimum of a half a year of training. It is common to see normal trainees grading just once each year from P3 and up.

When they reach the level of G2, students do the real fighting while wearing protective gear.

Some organizations start sparring when the student begins training. The International Kapap Association will start from the beginning level with full contact and minimal gear on the ground and stand up fighting. They use semi-professional MMA rules to keep people safe. Sparring needs to always be monitored and supervised by an instructor.

From the very beginning, the concept of Krav Maga was taking the simplest and most practical techniques of different fighting styles like street fighting, wrestling, and boxing and make them quickly teachable to the military. From this, Krav Maga has its base built in street fighting, wrestling, and Western boxing.

Krav Maga's philosophy puts emphasis on simultaneous offensive and defensive maneuvers and aggression. It has been used by regular infantry units, security apparatus, and Israel Defense Forces' Special Forces units. Other variations have been adopted and developed by Israeli intelligence and law enforcement organizations. There are many different organizations that teach different forms of Krav Maga all over the world like the United States Marine Corps and the British SAS.

Krav Maga in the Hebrew language is translated as contact combat. The word Krav simply means combat and the word Maga means contact.

Krav Maga tells its students to stay away from confrontation. If that isn't possible or could lead to harm, it tells its students to finish a fight as aggressively and quickly as possible. Training isn't limited to techniques to stay away from severe injury. They are aimed at the vulnerable body parts. Some techniques can cause permanent injury or even death.

Students will learn how to defend themselves against a variety of attacks. They are taught to counter these attacks the most efficient and quickest way possible.

Krav Maga ideas include:

- Seeing how important it is and learning to expand on the instinctive responses while under stress.

- Stay aware of your surroundings while you deal with threats so you can look for an escape route, other attackers, and objects that can be used to hit an opponent.

- Using easy and simple strikes that are repeatable.

- Targeting the attack on the vulnerable parts of the body like the liver, fingers, foot, knee, ribs, groin, solar plexus, face, throat, neck, eyes, and so forth.

- Use whatever object is at hand to hit your opponent.

- Attack before the opponent can and counterattack as quickly as possible.

- Continue striking your opponent until they are totally incapacitated.

- Develop physical aggression and realizing that physical aggression is the most crucial part of the fight.

- Simultaneous defense and attack.

Training might cover the development and study of situational awareness in order to understand a person's surroundings. You will learn to understand the mind and behavior of street confrontations. You will be able to identify any threats before attacks can occur. It could cover ways to handle the verbal and physical methods to stay away from violence when you can. It will teach mental toughness by using controlled fights to strengthen their mentality, so students will learn to control their impulses and don't do anything rash. Learn to attack only when it is a last resort or totally necessary.

Krav Maga is constantly evolving so it can reflect experiences in the everyday world. It isn't easy to specify a universal system as might be the case in some of the eastern martial arts. Within in the major Krav Maga organizations that are throughout the entire world, techniques are very similar.

Adopted techniques

Most of the techniques focus on instincts and effectiveness when under stress. Krav Maga is a system that isn't trying to replace any existing techniques. It takes what is most useful from all available systems. Some examples are:

- Ground work – per Brazilian Jiu-jitsu

- Throws and takedowns – per freestyle wrestling and judo

- Strikes – per boxing and Muay Thai

Techniques that have been taken from these systems have been modified to show that their beginnings were in a sport that had rules. This limits show how effective they are in real situations. Besides this, Krav Maga has figured out different supplementary techniques as was needed.

Examples of these types of techniques:

Escapes from holds and chokes:

- As stated above, most systems that allow take-down, chokes, and holds are competitive sports that don't allow strikes.

- Krav Maga then develops escapes that have been taken from these like strikes including headbutts, groin strikes, and foot stomps.

Empty hand defense includes:

- Pistol disarm.

- Defending against a person with a stick.

- Defending against a person with a knife.

Since there isn't any universal authority within this system, students might find that different schools use different techniques.

Since Imi Lichtenfeld created Krav Maga, many different organizations have been founded by former students.

The most popular are:

- In 1989 the Israeli Krav Magen Association or KAMI was created by Eli Avikzar.

- In 1997 the European Federation of Krav Maga or FEKM was founded by Richard Douieb. As of 2017, they have over 18,000 members in 12 different countries.

- In 1996 the International Krav Maga Federation or IKMF was founded.

- In 1983, Krav Maga Worldwide which was formerly known as the Krav Maga Association of America by Darren Levine and his best students.

- Darren Levine co-founded Fit to Fight with Ryan Hoover who is a second-degree black belt.

- Kobi Lichtenstein founded the South American Federation of Krav Maga.

- In 2005, Ioannis Papavlachopoulos founded Hellenic Krav Maga Federation or HKMF in Greece.

- In 2009, Rosario Citarda founded Italian Academy of Krav Maga or AIKM in Italy.

- In 2010, Eyal Yanilov founded Krav Maga Global or KMG.

- In 2010, Tsahi Shemesh who is an Expert 2 under the instructor Gabi Noah founded Krav Maga Experts or KME.

Krav Maga is a dynamic, modern, and effective fighting and self-defense system. It was designed to be intuitive and practical for people of any size, shape, and age. These techniques use your natural instincts to learn skills effectively and quickly while allowing you to address an attack under all scenarios. You will be taught how to defend your loved ones and yourself and gain awareness of your instinctive reflexes.

Part of the philosophy of Krav Maga is the easiest way to win when faced with a fight is to not get into a fight. We then spend too much time figuring out how to de-escalate a situation and win with avoidance. If a conflict is unavoidable, Krav Maga will teach us how to use whatever is at hand to neutralize the threat and remain calm.

Krav Maga is a striking and self-defense system. There aren't any showcases or competitions for self-defense. Krav Maga trains us to survive and avoid worst case scenarios. If you are being threatened by someone, you will learn how to avoid the entire scenario. If it is too far gone, you will be taught how to use the best techniques and strikes to win all while under a lot of stress. There aren't any absolutes or choreographies. There aren't any traditions and uniforms. Krav Maga isn't trained to help anyone start a fight or to show off. Training is to save lives of loved ones and ourselves. To quote Imi Lichtenfeld, Krav Maga is taught "so that one may walk in peace."

There is no experience needed to start Krav Maga. You will begin with learning the basic defense against attacks like headlocks and chokes, learning how to fall and get up, striking, and stances. You will also learn prevention and awareness techniques, how to deal when being attacked, and how to perform under stress. These will help keep you out of problem situations.

Once you've mastered the basics, students will learn how to deal with multiple attackers, complicated situations, weapons, and learn advanced weapon and combative techniques for being on the ground or standing.

For beginners, P1 classes are perfect for your first class. The material is rotated constantly, and there is no set rotation or introductory class. Most students practice all the material successfully after 35 classes which will take about four months to get ready for the P1 test to get to the rank of P2. It can become intense to join a class that is already in session, but it's all part of training. Self-defense is training under extreme and upsetting circumstances. If you want the ability to be able to react calmly during harsh times, it is crucial that your training is done with stress. Just participate and do the best you can. Every size, shape, and age can learn skills that could save your or someone else's life with Krav Maga training.

If you have experience in other martial arts, you will be asked to join the P1 class. The purpose and material differ from other martial arts until your instructor approves your advance.

Krav Maga provides the best self-defense training that focuses on realistic scenarios with quality attention and instruction. Classes are fun, ego-free, serious, and safe. All Krav Maga instructors are professional, certified, and have been trained by the best.

Basic Movements

We have to stand before we can even think about walking.

We all need to get back to basics every once in a while. We need to focus on our foundation that we build ourselves on. When you are learning to defend yourself, that foundation would be the fighting stance.

We have to learn a position that gives us the best flexibility, strength, and balance. We need to be able to defend against any attack and counter it with the abilities we get from the stance we have for fighting. We need to have the ability to quickly adapt and move at whatever danger we find ourselves in.

The best stance is one that is easy to get into, and that feels comfortable to you. By just taking a normal step forward with your leg that isn't dominant, you will be putting your feet in a comfortable position. Your weight needs to be balanced on the balls of your feet. This makes the moves more explosive when the time is right and will help you go in whatever direction is necessary. Next, you need to tuck your chin in and bring up your hands to protect your face.

This is called the home base. From this position, you will be able to plan your escape, assess the situation and area, gain distance, defend, and strike. You need to understand that anything could happen and the conditions of the situation will command the course of action. From the right fighting stance, we will give ourselves the best chance of getting safely out of any dangerous situation.

All Krav Maga moves have instinctive elements to them. They are easier to learn and faster to recall if you find yourself in due stress. We need a goal to establish self-defense on impulse. When reality sets in and you finally realize what you are doing, you will be halfway into your moves.

Besides teaching lifesaving skills, it can also be a wonderful confidence booster. It is also a great workout. Some get scared and intimidated when they see a class. Then reality hits and they see that they can actually do these moves. They finish a class and feel more self- assured and powerful.

Fundamentals
Krav Maga emphasizes basic techniques of street fighting that involves scratching, biting, knees, elbow strikes, kicks, and punches. You will learn the basic Krav Maga stance which is a relaxed boxing position in which your legs are placed shoulder width apart with one slightly in front of the other, so your stronger foot is in front and ready to go.

Six Pillars
Krav Maga was established on six pillars starting with learning how to attack and defend. Other strategies include focusing on the vulnerable spots like the groin, knee, throat, nose, and eyes. Using a continuous and fast combat motions that are designed to overtake the attacker before he can react. By being prepared and using decisive actions and doing whatever it takes to overthrow the threat. When you can, try some

techniques that will subdue the opponent before the violence can escalate. This is a process where you master just one move at a time and build on that one to make a whole arsenal of moves to have when you need them.

Four Steps for Action

If you are attacked or threatened, Krav Maga can teach you to process steps quickly so you can choose the right response as fast as possible. The first is recognizing the threat and summing up how much in danger you really are. Next comes analyzing the situation, evaluating your opponent, surroundings, and your position. Then you will need to decide if it will be better to act or not. If you decide to act, you must decide quickly what plan of action you are going to take.

Personal Weapons

The underlying principle of Krav Maga is using your body as a weapon against your attacker. Or you can use whatever object is at your disposal. You will learn how to do finger and elbow strikes, fist, roundhouse, or hand punches, different kinds of kicks that can come from the rear, side, and front. It teaches you how to do a fall without hurting yourself and a combination of methods to get yourself out of headlock and chokeholds both on the ground and standing.

Defense Against Guns and Knives

Krav Maga will teach you how to escape from an opponent with a knife by kicking and deflecting while staying away from the knife and moving away more to be able to kick more. Krav Maga has methods to defend against gunmen, where you use your body and hands to get out of the line of fire and will allow you to take the weapon and launch a counterattack with kicks and punches. Krav Maga methods could help in these deadly situations; you need to complete more advanced training before attempting these moves.

How to Get into the Proper Stance

There are two stances in Krav Maga: the fighting and the neutral stance. In the neutral stance, you will be facing your attacker with your feet lined up. Your hands will be raised in front of you ready to defend. This stance is designed to deploy your four weapons: two fists and two feet in a way that will ensure equal power and can reach with both sides of your body. The main difference is the fighting stance is an aggressive one. It will state that you are ready to fight where the neutral stance is nonaggressive one that gives you the element of surprise or an opening to defuse the situation.

Figure out your dominant side. This is called orthodox. You will eventually learn to do every technique from your offhand stance. Your dominant side will usually be the side you write with. If you are lucky and happen to be ambidextrous, then just begin as righty since most Krav Maga methods are taught right handed.

To position your body, stand square with your opponent. Your hips and shoulders need to be lined up with their hips and shoulders. You don't want your upper body off kilter as this makes your back hand strong and slow and your front hand useless. If you are squared correctly, then your cross and jab will have the power to knock your opponent out.

Proper foot placement is important. In this stance, if you can do it properly, you will have the ability to deliver powerful kicks from both legs. Your feet need to be shoulder width apart. Pretend you have skis on and the front of them are touching your attacker's toes.

- If you are right-handed, you left foot needs to be about a half step in front of your right foot.

- If you are left-handed, then do the opposite of the above.

- Bend your knees slightly and be up on your toes with both feet. You will be able to pivot quickly in this manner, change your level by squatting or jump forward and backward. Your toes need to be pointing toward your attacker at all times.

- You need to put around 60 percent of your weight on your back foot and about 40 percent on the front foot. Don't keep your legs in a straight line one in front of the other toward your opponent. This is just like keeping your balance on a balance beam and your kicks from the back leg will be slow and will remove all ability to kick with the leg in front.

Keep your elbows down and your hands up all the time. The only time this changes is if you throw a punch of your own. This will be followed by a quick recoil back to the start position. You can check the height of your hands by touching your thumbs to your cheeks. They need to be here to protect your jaw. Elbows need to be pointed down to protect your liver and ribs from punches to your body and sharp weapons. Yes, it is going to hurt to get cut on your elbow, but it won't be as bad as being stabbed and your guts spilling out.

Your chin needs to stay down. Keep your chin tucked just like you are holding a towel with your chin. You need to keep looking up as if you are looking through your forehead. This will protect your chin from incoming punches. They might punch you in the top of your head, but the joke's on them since this is an extremely hard part of your head and it will probably break their hand.

Round your shoulders forward and shrug them up. This brings them around your chin. If your attacker throws a punch that you don't see coming. If a second attacker that you didn't see tries to get you in a headlock, your shoulders will absorb most of the impact and prevent them from getting under your chin. This will help protect your throat from a slash from a knife.

Here are some easy self-defense moves:

Front Kick to the Groin
This maneuver works because the groin is an area that can't be conditioned to be stronger. This makes it vulnerable to attacks. A hard kick to the groin can cause nausea and abdominal pain. In other words,

your opponent will double over in pain, and this leaves you the opportunity to run away.

Here is how to do this move: Stand with feet a bit wider than hip width apart. Face your attacker. Your left leg is slightly forward and your right leg is slightly behind you. Bring your arms into your chest as if you are blocking a punch. Figure out how high your opponent's groin is. Bring your right leg and lead with your knee. Your hips will pivot toward the opponent to get power from the core as you bring your leg up forcefully. As you raise your leg up, flick your lower leg, so your shin or foot makes contact with the groin. Now, recoil to the beginning stance so you can defend yourself or run away.

Hammer Punch

If you haven't thrown a punch before, hitting with your knuckles can cause you to break your hand. You will be better off using the hammer punch. This is a very easy maneuver to learn and recall in stressful times.

How to do this stance: Stand in normal fighting stance, with arms protecting chest. Your dominant hand will be in a fist. Rotate the hips just a bit toward your opponent and raise the dominant hand up. Bend your arm at the elbow like you are getting ready to throw a ball. Now, move forward quickly with your hips and bring the arm down and smack your opponent in the face with the bottom part of the fist. Recoil to the normal stance and get ready to give another blow or run away.

Getting Out of a Headlock from Behind

Being attacked from behind is scary since you can't see or strike at them with your strength straight away. This technique will allow you to remove their forearm from your throat and get out of the headlock. When you can finally face your opponent, you can deliver a blow to the face if needed.

How to do this maneuver: If your opponent has their right arm around your neck, put both your hands on their forearm and hand. Duck your head to the left. Now, press your left shoulder into your opponent's chest so you can get some space between your bodies. Last, bring your left foot between your bodies. You should be able to get your head under your opponent's arm and get free.

Getting Out of a Frontwards Chokehold

This can be done by someone who is smaller than their attacker. If there is somebody choking you from the front, your main goal is to get their hands off of you. This move uses momentum and speed to overthrow their strength. This technique needs to be paired with a kick to the groin to keep the opponent from getting more aggressive.

How to do this maneuver: Raise your arms to the sides and bend them into what looks like hooks. Bring your hands up into the middle of your attacker's arms and push their wrists off of your throat. Grab their thumbs and remove their hands by violently twisting their wrists away from you. Your back muscles need to be braced while doing this move.

Getting Out of a One-Hand Chokehold While Against a Wall

An opponent will use one hand to grab and hold you by the throat while pushing you against the wall behind you.

This attack is done to make you comply with the opponent's will. If you can pretend as if you are complying and are non-resistant can give you an advantage of getting in the first blow. You have to get free of this position fast, so your opponent doesn't have time to use the other hand to choke harder or grab a weapon.

How to do this maneuver: Tuck your chin into your chest. Put pressure on your opponent's thumb to weaken the hold. Bring your hands up and grab your opponent's wrist. Use your nondominant hand and grab their wrist close to the thumb and pluck it from your throat and drive it toward the ground. At the same time bring up your dominant hand to hit your opponent's nose, throat, or jaw. Now rotate your hips into the blow to add momentum and force to the hit to make it more powerful. Knee your opponent in the groin and hit the soft spots.

Disarm a Knife-to-Throat from Behind

An opponent has placed a blade against your throat from behind while their other hand is controlling your arm and limiting your movements.

Having a knife against your throat is a great convincer since the danger is so imminent. Most people will do anything to stay away from it. This is why this type of attack is so prevalent.

How to do this maneuver: Pretend to comply with your opponent's demands. Don't resist any movements because your throat can get accidentally cut. In a quick motion, put both hands on the wrist that is holding the knife and bring their arm down. Keep it tight against your chest. Drop the whole of your weight down while tucking your chin and look at the blade. This will move the threat from the throat to the face. This will still hurt but won't be as deadly. Use the hand that is nearer to the opponent to hit them in the groin and quickly brings it back to their wrist. Their arm will still be around your neck with your hands pinning their wrist into your chest. Tuck your head under the closest armpit and keep your chin down and their wrist that is holding the knife secured. Pivot your body and feet, so you are on the opponent's side instead of in front of them. Stomp on your opponent's foot that is closest to you and push them down on the ground.

Stomp Kick to the Groin

When an opponent knees or kicks you in the groin or midsection, this can lead to follow-up attacks, pain, and severe damage.

This will work with other defensive moves as well, but if your opponent kicks out with their right leg, you will defend yourself with your left hand. Remember to mirror your attacker. By doing this, your arm stays straight, so your forearm will create the maximum protection and coverage. You will swing your arm across your body like a windshield wiper.

How to do this maneuver: As the opponent bring their leg up toward your groin, use your hand to divert the leg by using the windshield swipe movement. You will use the entire length of the arm to do this. Don't grab their leg. Step to the side away from their leg. This momentum will put you to the opponent's back or side. Strike their face with a closed fist after the block.

Defensive Scenarios

There are many ways to defend yourself against attackers using Krav Maga. This chapter will cover how to defend yourself against an attacker with a knife, gun, and chair. If you have not been properly trained in Krav Maga, your best defense is going to be a good offense. It isn't shameful to run away from a dangerous situation. Your life is more important than bragging rights. If you must fight, here are some pointers on how to unarm your attacker.

Knife Defense

There are several types of knife defense. There are the Filipino styles of Escrima, Kali, and Arnis. You could learn to use a stick against a knife. Systema, Kung fu, Ninjitsu, Jujitsu all have knife defenses, and they are all good techniques. You need to figure out if knife defense suits the circumstances in your life.

Wearing full protective gear is the best way to train in knife defense, hiding the knife behind your back, and attacking with a sudden burst. This will mimic reality.

Know your weapon so you can defend against the weapon. You need to be able to fight with the weapon. This is what is called reality knife defense. This does apply to guns, batons, or any edged or blunt weapons. Many schools that teach martial arts just teach defense. If you don't know how an attacker is going to use the weapon, you have no idea how to disarm them of it.

Some practitioners hold onto style loyalty where they think their style is the only one that works. They can't get out of their own head to realize they are hurting their students by not teaching them everything they need to know about defending themselves on the streets. To teach this way just shows that they haven't faced real fear. If they had, they wouldn't care what technique they use or if it was used by the ancient Hebrews, Native American Indians, or your best friend's grandmother. All that matter is whether or not it works. Remember that in reality knife defense you must ask yourself what is going to keep me alive on the streets?

Learn the Attack

Most schools teach defense methods first before they teach how to fight with a weapon. That puts understanding on how you want to defend not on the possibilities of how a criminal might attack. Most Aikido classes teach one correct way to attack, and all the defense moves were based around that attack. No one thought to ask what is going to happen if the attacker didn't do that certain move. Most devoted disciples dare not ask, is the real knife defense?

Before we can figure out the solution, such as blocking the maneuver, doing an evasive movement, and a counter, we have to identify the problem better known as the nature of the attack.

We need to know what could happen. We need to learn from people who have experienced this first hand. You can get advice from anyone that has faced an encounter face to face. This doesn't compare with the first-hand experience and don't go into a bar asking for a fight with a drunken opponent so you can get in some practice.

Most of the knife disarms don't work since they deal with grabbing the knife. Most gang members know this and will rub their arms down with Vaseline. Some will wear spikes on their wrists, so a normal karate block will cause you to get stabbed. If you ignore this information, just stay inside your safe little dojo.

Figure Out Where the Knife Is

Most traditional knife disarms are done by taking the person down, pushing down the arm and lowering them onto the ground. Many don't consider that many criminals will hide knives in their boots. By placing them on the ground puts them in the perfect position to grab the knife and stab you. If they hit the right place, they could cut an artery and cause you to bleed out. This won't happen in a dojo, but it can and has happened on the streets. Be knowledgeable.

Know Your Surroundings

Some practitioners in the Filipino styles carry two knives and are extremely proficient with them. Maybe we need to put an emphasis on this within our training.

Simple answer, no. We are a gun society. Many assailants aren't master swordsman; they are just angry killers that will grab a knife and want to kill. They haven't had years of training.

Even if they manage to stab a couple of people by catching them off guard, they could easily be taken down by a citizen that knows what they are doing and can unarm this person. This is why we put an emphasis on knife defense.

Not many people have the time or want to become master knife fighters. This takes years. We get trained in what is called high percentage moves. We attack the arm that is holding the knife aggressively and hard. We make it painful. At the same time, we hit them in their face or vulnerable part of their body. Beginners think that "if they do this, then I can do that." In reality, no you won't because you have already put them in a lot of pain. Once the arm is hit and we move on to the face and body hitting it aggressively and continuing to hit with elbow and knee strikes, it will effectively shut them down. It's not going to be picture perfect, but it is effective.

One of Bruce Lee's top disciples, Danny Inosanto stated that "Knife disarm is incidental if not accidental." Many schools of martial arts just continue to work on fancy ways to disarm your opponent.

Bruce Lee said it best, "Absorb what is useful, reject what is useless, cultivate what is truly your own."

Defending Against a Gun

You are walking down the street and all of a sudden someone is standing in front of you holding a gun. What do you do? There are several techniques to use to disarm a criminal. They are all dangerous. Check out the situation to see if you can reduce the threat in another way.

Take the Gun from Your Opponent

The main goal in this situation is to save your life. Fighting back does increase the odds that you will lose your life.

- If you aren't professionally trained by extensive martial arts, the police or the military in how to disarm an attacker, the safest bet if faced with a gun is just to do what they say. The only exception here is never getting into a vehicle with them. You are putting your life on the line; this isn't the movies. In most cases, your opponent has more experience in this situation than you do.

- The mistake that is made by most victims is over confidence. This has led to many deaths. The second mistake is fighting back. There may be times that you might figure out that you have to.

Grab their wrist. If you have figured out the only thing to do is to disarm the attacker because you will be shot anyway, turn the gun away from you. This is extremely dangerous. Don't attempt this if you haven't been trained unless it is irrevocably a necessity.

- You have to make sure the gun is away from your body as you grab and spin it away.

- Continue this energy that you have created by twisting their arm around you to your right as you turn away from where they were positioned originally. Now, flip them onto the ground as you spin right continuing to hold the attacker's arm.

- Keep your hands on their arm, and get the gun from them. You could also step over them and hold their arm with your knee.

Take the gun out of their hand. Rotate the gun toward the ground and break their fingers as you do so. The attacker's finger is going to be on the trigger.

- Rotate the gun to the right. Remember these maneuvers are extremely dangerous especially if the criminal is bigger and stronger than you. You also risk the gun firing and hitting innocent people in the area.

- Remove the gun from their broken hand. Use your right hand to hold their wrist. Now take your left hand and bend their wrist. Take hold of the gun and push it down. This is extremely important. If you don't take hold of their wrist before rotating the gun downward, you are going to let them keep the gun.

If a gun is pointed at your back, you can disarm the assailant by turning around and stepping in and then under their arm. Then rip the gun out of their hands.

- You can do either of these things next: you can twist the gun in their hand and break their fingers or rip the gun from their hand. Move your left hand to the side of the gun and simultaneously move your body to your opponent's right.

- When you put your left hand on the side of the assailant's gun, take a counterclockwise circular step to the right in between their feet and turn the gun toward them.

- Take your wrist and lock the assailant's right hand. Turn the gun to the assailant's throat. Take them to the ground. The goal of these moves is to reposition the gun before taking it from their hand.

Take control of the weapon. You have to get control of the weapon so your assailant can't point it at you. This is going to happen extremely fast, and they are going to try to take control.

- Move forward extremely fast. Place your weight in and down on the gun. You need to get the weapon down and in to limit the attacker's ability to move it. Move your feet to constantly put weight on the weapon it doesn't matter what the attacker does.

- You are going to use your body weight and hip muscles to torque the assailant's wrist and take them down. In one fluid movement, put pressure on their wrist and force them onto the ground at the same time take control of the weapon. At this point, you can further incapacitate your assailant by kicking them in the head, groin, or midsection.

- If the assailant has a shotgun or rifle, reach over their shoulder and grasp the gun's butt stock. Insert your right hand with your thumb pointed at the ground and grasp the weapon's barrel. Pull the weapon toward you forcefully to weaken their leverage and yank it upward. Pull the weapon away from the attacker.

Prevent a Shooting

Give them what they want. It will be less deadly if you comply with their demands as long as it doesn't threaten your life.

- If an assailant wants your purse, wallet, or car, give it to them. Throw whatever they asked for behind them. They should go after it, and this gives you an opening to run away.

- There are some instances where the assailant gets what they asked for, and they shoot the victim anyway. There isn't any surefire way to get out of a dangerous situation.

Change the line of fire. The easiest way in defending yourself is to eliminate the biggest threat. If the gun is pointing at your, this is the biggest danger to you.

- You have to get yourself out of the line of fire. This is done by moving either yourself or the gun. Make this first movement as undetectable and small as possible. If you make too big of a move or try to step away, you might cause the assailant to discharge their weapon.

- Use your hand to change the line fire so that it will hit fewer vital parts. Move it laterally in the shortest possible line. If it is pointing at your heart, move it either right, left, or up.

Run. This can be dangerous since the assailant could shoot you in the back.

- If you choose to do this, try throwing something like a purse, wallet or keys over the assailant, so they have to turn around to get it. Run in the opposite direction in either an unpredictable or zigzag pattern.

- This is extremely dangerous. But to be fair, everything about this situation is dangerous. Just comply with their demands as best as you can. If you haven't been seen, just run in the opposite direction and hide. If you are found, then you can fight.

Let your intentions be known. If you aren't ready to make your move, make your intentions clear to the gunman before you move.

- Say, "I am reaching into my pocket to get my wallet" before you actually do it.

- Watch the assailant as you do this. Find identifying marks about them that will help the police find them later.

Get the assailant's mind on something else. If you are facing an assailant that doesn't want anything else but to shoot you, there are a few things you can try to distract them.

- Get away from the area or building. Run away, if you can.

- If running isn't an option, hide. Put your phone on silent and barricade yourself inside a room. Make sure you barricade the door well before you call 9-1-1.

- If you are found, fight. Use what is within reach, books, computers, chairs, tables, etc. Throw them or hit the assailant with them. This would be better with a group of people, but it works alone, too. The main goal is to take down the assailant.

- Find a group and band together. Grab the gun and twist it away from your body fast. Keep your hold on the gun even when they try to take it back. Push your entire body weight forward and hit them in the throat or the face as hard as you can. Grab the non-shooting end of the gun. Kick the assailant in the groin. Twist your hands so that you break the assailant's finger in the trigger guard.

Throw the Criminal Off

Act passive and scared and raise your hands. The assailant might not harm you if you don't provoke them. If you are planning on disarming the assailant, just act deferential and passive to throw them off.

- You just need to comply. You don't have to try anything that could risk your lives.

- Act as passive and cooperative as possible. Say, "I'm not asking for trouble. What can I do for you?" Give them the impression you aren't a threat to them.

- Keep your hands above the gun but don't keep them still. Wave them around to get into the assailant's peripheral vision to hide your defensive movements that you are getting ready to make.

Get at least an arm's length away from the gun. In a quick movement, first, move your head, and grab the gun.

- Pivot the gun away from you. Twist the assailant's wrist. Change their focus with a kick, punch, or both.

- Put your free hand on the hammer but know where the barrel is pointing. As you knee, stomp or kick the assailant keep both hands firmly on the gun. With the assailant's wrist twisted, and both hands holding the gun firmly, rip the gun from their hands. You now have possession of the gun.

When you now have the gun take some steps back. The best thing to do once you have possession of the gun is to get away without having to use it.

- Run away with the gun. If the assailant continues to come after you, you might not have a choice. Check the gun by tapping the magazine to make sure it is in.

- Draw attention to yourself by making noise and screaming. Hopefully, the assailant runs away. The goal here isn't firing the gun. Learn the laws about self-defense. In most cases, if you are in imminent danger of bodily harm or death, you are entitled to defend yourself.

Stay calm. Don't panic or you might make your assailant panic, and this makes the situation more dangerous.

- Keep a psychological advantage. Keep eye contact. This forces them to see you as a person, and it might be harder for them to shoot you. Don't make the game challenging or intimidating.

- Figure out what the assailant is up to. Why are they holding a gun on you? If their motive is robbery, then they might not want to kill you. If you are caught in the middle of a mass shooting where the intent of the assailant is to harm as many people as they can, this is totally different. If you aren't sure they want to kill you, you can hope they spare your life.

Don't put yourself into a dangerous situation. You can lessen the chances of having to use self-defense.

- Never walk alone, if you are impaired, a female, or at night. Criminals look for vulnerable people, and they pounce on the opportunity. If you are walking down the road and staggering drunk, you might become a target. Never flash jewelry or money.

- Take notice of your surroundings. Don't distract yourself by using your cell phone or walking with your head down. Notice what is going on around you all the time. Try to wear shoes that will let you run if needed.

- You can get a conceal-carry permit if it is allowed in your state and you get properly trained. If you are in college, at work, or at your apartment, ask for a security escort if they are available. Carry pepper spray or mace if it's legal in your area.

Defending a Two-Handed Overhead Chair Attack

Let's find out how to defend yourself against an opponent with a stool, chair or other object coming at you with an overhead attack.

Lessen the distance between your opponent and you by aligning your deflecting hand with a body lean forward, bury your chin in your shoulder. Go toward your opponent quickly with the opposite leg of your deflecting arm. Your hand will hit just above the opponent's closest hand that is holding the chair.

While the chair glides overhead, take a step forward with your back leg without breaking contact with your deflecting arm on the opponent's arm. The attack will once again glide along your arm. It will go past your shoulder. Then it will just glance off your back.

Turn your deflecting arm's hand in and move it around your opponent's arm. Take control of the chair with this arm.

At the same time counterattack with punches or elbow strikes using your free arm. Combine this with strikes from your knee.

If you can't snare both of your opponent's arms, you have to get control of his far arm by grabbing it in an overhand grip. Just watch the opponents near arm to make sure they don't release control of the chair to their far arm. They could use this to attack you with a whip or backhanded attack. Don't forget to continuously attack your opponent.

If you get control of the chair, use it as a weapon of opportunity and use the chair as a weapon.

If you both have control of the chair, kick it out of the way. Kicking the chair out of the way doesn't violate Krav Maga's principle of controlling the weapon. You are controlling the weapon by kicking it out of the way. If someone else picks up the chair to attack you, use a control technique to put the first opponent in the line of fire. You might have to defend yourself against another attack would be the worst-case scenario. You might also disable the opponent who might drop the chair. This will let you pick it up and use it as a weapon.

Unarmed Assaults

We've covered several types of armed attacks. Let's look at some unarmed attacks and see what is the best way to get out of them. Here are some ways you can deal with, avoid, and prevent violent attacks:

- Know the situation – You need to understand and focus as fast as you possibly can what the nature of the confrontation is.

- Figure out the opponent's intentions – You need to make eye contact, read your opponent's body language and face him with your hands high. This will put you in a great starting point. Your main goal is to have the upper hand in every situation.

- Avoidance – You need to keep your distance from your opponent. It doesn't matter if the person is seven feet tall, or a young child, distance is the critical factor.

- Prevention – Stopping the progress of violence early is critical. Here are three rules pertinent to this situation:

  o The easiest way is to run away if at all possible.

  o Find an object nearby to threaten your opponent or use to defeat the opponent physically or mentally.

- o Keep the situation from happening in the first place without making any contact. If you are surrounded or forced, then acting quickly is the easiest way to defeat your opponent.

- Preemptive attacks – There are different attacks you can use to prevent your opponent from hurting you or getting to you. Use these when:

  - o You figure out the intentions of your opponent.

  - o You know that danger is real and immediate.

  - o There are no other alternatives for you.

- Compliance and Submission – If you use body language that tells your attacker that you are complying with them while keeping your head and knowing you need to leave as quickly as you can, is sometimes the best thing you can do. Submission works if the opponent wants to dominate, usually you might suffer just a bit of damage if any at all. You may lose the battle and suffer some embarrassment, but you won't suffer any physical harm.

  Compliance works when the opponent is looking for more resources, for example, if you are being robbed, give the robber what he wants. The proper way to commence and give compliance has to be practiced and learned.

If you feel that submission or compliance will just not work for you during an incident, you need to either start with the right aggressive reactions or use fake behaviors and attack if you can.

- Looking for assistance – The most important thing you need to consider is looking for assistance. Yes, I said look for help. Seeking help from others may allow you to overcome the opponent's bad intentions.
  However, you won't always find yourself with the ability to call for help. In this case, you need to be aware of your surrounding and watch the opponent's moves very closely.

The normal assumption is always "it is up to me to act; nobody else can do it for me." If someone offers to help, by all means, let them. You just became very lucky.

- Doing the right technique – Using the correct tactics and techniques of Krav Maga is important. You have to know just when to use them. You must be aware of the right time and place. You must be in the correct physical and mental state. By doing this, you will be more balanced and have the ability to manage the fight. Exploit this to your advantage. This will give you the upper hand to be able to take control of any situation. Stay focused. Try to neutralize all distractions and disturbances.

- Avoid illegal consequences – Just because you are being attacked doesn't give you the right to do what you want when it comes to using rocks, your fist, or firearms. You should try to de-escalate the situation and try to leave before it gets to that point. We have to act within the law, and the use of weapons and tools against an opponent is the hardest decision we have to make when we are able to get control of the situation. So, acting wisely and using the right Krav Maga techniques against an opponent is a critical step when faced with a fight.

- Let others know – If there are people around, let them know about the situation as quickly as you can. This is the smartest move you can do especially if you are actively defending and counterattacking. Because you are the victim, when you get possession of the weapon, use it if you can or hide it so that you won't stand out.

- Get to a safe place – Your body needs to process the situation after an attack, so, getting to a safe place is the best thing for you. Deep pains and injuries can be life threatening if they don't get taken care of as quickly as humanly possible after an attack. When you have reached your safe place, you need to check your body status and look for any injuries and treat them accordingly.

Call for help as soon as you can. Remember as many details as you can from the event like the attacker's looks, what they were wearing, if he was driving a car, etc. We need to be able to identify your attacker so they can be apprehended.

- Keep in mind – We have to defend ourselves any way we can. It might be with our minds, a weapon, or our hands. We have to be more efficient, better, and smarter. Stay away from the opponent and apply any needed technique that you have been educated and trained to do. Use the post-fight tactics like:

    o Leave as quickly as you can

    o Assist and locate family and friends

    o Locate and search for tools that could help you in the fight

    o Look for and aim to get to an exit

    o Search for your things like phone, car keys, and papers

Standing Side Headlock Escape

A side headlock is a great way to learn how to end an attack properly. This doesn't mean that the headlock is the end. Nobody puts another human being in a headlock to just hold them forever. A large part of this time is just a transitional phase. A headlock is usually used to hold the person still for punches. It can be used to take someone to the ground. If the person knows what they're doing, it can be used to choke them out. In these instances, the end of the headlock was to suffocate, move, or control. You can look at these as just a school yard or bully attack.

If a person gets you in a real headlock, their hips will be in front of yours. This will upset your center of gravity, and this makes it easy to manipulate you. You will need to take a huge step around to get your hips in line with theirs. You need to be so close that your groin is touching their thigh. The lower part of your body will be slightly squatting when you step around them. They won't be able to toss you to the ground if you can be fast enough with your moves. If the person putting you in a headlock is fast, they can get you in it and have you on the ground before you can ever react. That's okay. There are ways you can get out of it even on the ground. If you can, stay on your feet.

There are some reasons you need to stay on your feet: If your attacker is bigger and stronger than you, they can overpower you when they get you on the ground. You have to assume that the attacker has a friend nearby and will help them if they need it. They can easily stomp you if you are on the ground.

Once you are out of the headlock, there are some defensive moves you need to do. The slap and peel are next. When you take that huge step around your opponent, the hand that stayed in front of the opponent will slap upward as hard as you can and then into their groin. At the same time, the hand that is behind your opponent reaches up between both heads. At this point, you can either gouge at their eyes or grab their face. Your arm that has their face pull that elbow down to your waist. You are essentially trying to pull their head back and down. You will be stronger than their neck. You might not be as strong as their core. A solid downward pull toward your waist will have them at the perfect angle. If you can accomplish this quickly and hard enough, they will go to the ground. Pull as hard as you physically can. If they begin to resist in a way that causes you to struggle, continue to hit them in the groin with the other hand. Another successful tip here is just to grab the groin and pull with all your might. If pulling their neck isn't going the way you wanted, you can take the front arm and hit them in the chin to assist in getting their head back.

Be constantly aware of other threats. When you have cracked their grip off of your head, always look for ways to either counter attack or disengage. Move where you have scanned. Look for other attackers that could be in the area.

Krav Maga Moves All Women Need to Know

Krav Maga doesn't advocate beginning fights but was made to help you fill in the blanks that occur when you get scared or are under dire stress.

It will take time to build muscle memory; there are some moves that are easier to remember and keep in mind that will help you get yourself out of dangerous situations.

Here are six moves every woman needs to know:

Open Hand Strike

This will use the heel of your hand to hit the most vulnerable parts of your attacker's head like back and front of the neck, eyes, and face. Using a punch action can hurt your attacker. If you decide to go for their eyes, it is going to seriously bother them. Don't pull the arm all the way back. Keeping your elbow bent in front of your ribs will warn the attacker that more is coming.

Groin Kick

The groin is the most vulnerable spots on the body for both women and men. Know how much room you have. If you are farther away, try to aim where your toes or shoelaces will hit them. If you are close to them, use the knee. This is the one move all women need to know to defend against a male attacker.

Outside Defense or 360

Attackers will try to get to their targets from the side or behind by using a circle attack to punch, grab, or slap. To defend against this, intercept the hit by using the side of your wrist and hit them in the same way. Keep your arm at a right-angle to keep enough space between you and your opponent.

Handbag Grab

If your bag, hand, or arm is being pulled, the main thing here is moving with it and using their energy. Don't pull away and resist, use their energy to kick or hit them.

Attack from the Ground

If your attacker takes you down, figure out your distance and kick them. If they are standing above you, kick with both feet at one time. Thrust your hips up and off the floor to get more power. Once you have them away from you, get up and run as fast as you can.

Conclusion

Thanks for making it through to the end of *Krav Maga*. Let's hope it was informative and able to provide you with all of the tools you need to achieve your goals.

The next step is to take what you have read here and keep yourself from being a victim. Some of these maneuvers should only be done by a trained professional. If you don't totally understand how or what you are doing, you could do yourself more harm than good. It would be best if you found a studio near you that teaches the art of Krav Maga so you can get hands on instructions with a trained professional and become skilled in the art.

Finally, if you found this book useful in any way, a review on Amazon is always appreciated!

Made in the USA
Las Vegas, NV
02 November 2021